Inspiring Ideas
to Support Children's Interests

Susie Rosback, Natalie Coulson
& Lease Cowen

TEACHING
SOLUTIONS

Published in 2014 by TEACHING SOLUTIONS
PO Box 197, Albert Park 3206, Australia
Phone: +61 3 9636 0212
Fax: +61 3 9699 9242
Email: info@teachingsolutions.com.au
Website: www.teachingsolutions.com.au

Copyright © Susie Rosback, Natalie Coulson & Lease Cowan 2014

ISBN 978-1-925145-00-7

Illustrated by Tom Kurema
Cover design by Tom Kurema
Printed in China

11-2104

Contents

Chapter 1

Supporting learning and development

We have created this resource to be used by educators to stimulate their programs and provide fresh, innovative and creative ideas that support children's learning and development.

After researching many educators across a spectrum of different services Australia wide, we came up with nine areas of interest that are common to most children. We have also included a chapter on painting ideas because we strongly believe in supporting children's creativity and offering opportunities to use many different paint mediums and a variety of painting experiences.

Theme vs interest area

In the late 1990s and early this century the word 'theme' became less popular in describing program interest areas in early childhood. The concept of planning your program based on a 'theme' became a thing of the past. Instead it was recommended that early childhood should reflect the culture, context and interests of all the children attending the service.

If children's interests are to become the focal point of the program, then educators need to find different ways of discovering these interests and then planning for them. In the past, the program was planned – and that was what was taught. Now there is more pressure on educators to be able to change the direction of their planning to support the children's interests and to perhaps put aside other planned experiences to accommodate the ideas emerging from the group.

However, it is important to create balance in your planning. A program for young children should be neither solely child-centred nor solely educator-directed. A quality educational program will have a balance of both child-initiated and adult-led experiences. As education professionals it is vital that we understand the intention behind every aspect of our program. We need to have a thorough knowledge of the benefits and goals in all we offer children, but most importantly, we need to be able to articulate these ideas to colleagues and families attending our service.

Children's interests have not changed since the introduction of the EYLF and the learning outcomes. Back when we planned under developmental domains the interests were the same. It's just that now we have a perspective on learning that is occurring.

The main change comes from the educator's ability to discover these interests and then design their program in response. So, for example, an educator might have planned for one thing to occur in the program but if a child walks in with a caterpillar from the garden, the program might take a turn to the investigation of minibeasts.

This type of programming not only supports the emerging interests of each child, it also shows children that we respect them, that their ideas are important and that they are a valued member of the community, supporting their friends' learning as well as their own.

So in this book we cover, in detail, nine areas of interest or 'good old themes', but in a way that reflects the National Quality Standard and supports the acquisition of the learning outcomes outlined in the Early Years Learning Framework.

The idea is not that you set up your program according to these interest areas and then teach to them. Instead, the book is designed to provide you with a multitude of ideas so that when Charlie comes in with a rocket he made on the weekend, you can follow that interest and support his developing passion for learning in a variety of ways.

Discovering children's interests

There are many ways of uncovering the interests of the children you teach.

Family contributions

Families are a terrific source of information on their children's interests. This is especially helpful with children who are not yet talking or for those who are a bit shy. You can put a family contribution form near your sign-in area and parents can write directly on that. These ideas can provide you with weeks of stimulus for your program.

Group times

Another way to discover children's interests is through group-time discussions. By sitting together and sharing ideas, children learn from one another. They develop a love of learning and gain insight and interest in new things. Group times can uncover a multitude of terrific ideas that can be developed within the program. Many of these will lead to programming opportunities.

Then to extend the children's thinking further, I would google scarecrows and we would look at images of them online. From this we would talk about the features of our scarecrow. Then when we go outside, we would find what we need from the shed and create the scarecrow.

Informal discussion

When you are sitting with children talking as they play, you can uncover some incredible insights into their current interests, things going on in their lives and outings they may have been on that could all contribute to your program.

Sharing bag

By sending home a sharing bag, you give each child the opportunity to share things that interest them. These interests could inform the program and create wonderful learning opportunities for other children.

Extending the learning opportunities

Discussion ~ Questioning ~ Inspiration ~ Variety ~ Nature ~ Nurture ~ Listening ~ Respect

Extending children's learning opportunities is a vital part of developing a love of learning in the children you teach. A child presents an idea to the group, and you can either acknowledge the idea and move on with other conversation or you can ask questions, encourage thinking, do research and explore ideas to further extend the potential of that learning opportunity.

An example of this: We are talking about planting our vegetable garden and a child suggests we make a scarecrow. I could say, *Yes, that's a nice idea* and leave it at that ... or I could ask, *Why would we need a scarecrow? How could we make a scarecrow? Will it have a happy face? Has anyone ever seen a scarecrow?*

These opportunities will arise in your service many times each day. A child walks in with his shark book and wants to make a shark ... so you grab some chicken wire (always handy to have a roll in the shed) and start working on creating the body for a shark that will become a major project over a week of papier mache, paint and amazing investigations into different sharks.

A child wants to make a didgeridoo, and you provide them with a tube and some paint. Do you then walk away from that experience, or do you open a whole area of understanding about didgeridoos? *Who plays them? How are they played? How do we make sound by blowing into a tube …?* The opportunities are endless.

So, to be able to extend children's learning effectively you need to be interested in the conversations you have with children. Be willing to ask more questions and find out how much the children know. Be armed with the ability to undertake research where you don't know the answers yourself. Have IT equipment that supports your ability to respond to children's interests immediately.

Hypothesise ~ Reflect ~ Research ~ Discover ~ Inquire ~ Question ~ Discover ~ Investigate

Each time you meet with your children, get into the habit of asking them questions. *Why do you think that happened? How do you do that? What's happening right now? What can you see, smell, hear? How does it feel? If we do this … what will happen? How can we find out? Does anyone know?*

Children are a great source of knowledge and understanding of the world around them. They don't fear getting the answer wrong so they will just give it a go. Try to encourage any answer by saying *That's a great thought* or *I like your idea*. That way, children will feel confident to explore ideas further.

Do internet searches, and teach children how to use search engines wisely and effectively. It is great for them to know what they are and how we use them, and to enjoy the benefits of research and discovery.

Another way to extend thinking and learning in young children is to create inspiring play spaces that encourage creativity, autonomy and deeper thought in the area of interest. For example, placing children's literature near an experience (see chapter 11) encourages children to explore the ideas and extend play.

Using natural and manmade props together enables children to explore nature while directing creativity in a particular area. Using IT screens with interesting and beautiful pictures of things from the world around us, such as flowers, insects, space shuttles, diggers, trucks, ocean creatures, African animals ... helps children to observe detail and allows them to extend their creativity and imagination.

Extending creativity and development through discussion, by talking with children about the particular items of interest, will allow for further extension in learning opportunities.

A child who feels respected, and who knows that you listen to them intently and that they are a valued member of the community, will offer so much to the learning of the whole group. It is we, as educators, who need to develop our skills in extending children's learning, so that we can take these children to greater heights and ultimately develop a love of learning in the children we teach. That is the greatest gift we can give any child.

Chapter 2

The National Quality Standard

This book focuses on the programs educators offer, and the importance of building relationships with children, families and the community to provide better outcomes for children and greater opportunities for learning.

The National Quality Standard (NQS) consists of seven quality areas that outline how children's education and care services are to conduct themselves to create the best outcomes for children, and which services are assessed and rated against.

We feel that the standards and elements from the NQS listed below best illustrate the goals of the experiences shared in this book. They are listed here so you can refer to them when writing your programs and gain a deeper understanding of the value of the experiences you are offering.

1.1.5 **Every child is supported to participate in the program.**

By showing children that we respect their ideas and value their contributions, we support them to take part in the program. By focusing on common areas of interest there are always likely to be aspects of the program that will engage each child.

1.1.6 **Each child's agency is promoted, enabling them to make choices and decisions and influence events and their world.**

Children learn respect through behaviour that is modelled to them. If we listen intently to children's ideas and then work to support them in implementing these ideas, we show them that they are valued and capable of supporting the learning of the whole group.

1.2.2 **Educators respond to children's ideas and play and use intentional teaching to scaffold and extend each child's learning.**

By being 'deliberate, purposeful and thoughtful in their decisions and actions' (EYLF p. 45) educators can design programs based on their knowledge of child development, learning outcomes and the needs of the individual children in their care. The ability to use reflection, questioning, research and, above all, flexibility in thinking and implementation are the keys to scaffolding and extending each child's learning.

1.2.3 **Critical reflection on children's learning and development, both as individuals and in groups, is regularly used to implement the program.**

Critical reflection is the ability to look at the planned experiences as well as other aspects of the program and really work out what did and didn't work. We need to develop skills to devise different ways to achieve the outcomes and articulate what went wrong and why. Reflecting with colleagues and with children helps us to see things from different perspectives.

2.1 **Educators and coordinators are focused, active and reflective in designing and delivering the program for each child.**

The program you offer children will take much thought and preparation. It is important to reflect on the experiences you have on offer and on the conversations that arise throughout the day. Reflection can take many forms: a conversation with colleagues, your thoughts in relation to things going on in your room, parent feedback, a diary, observations, notes and your program plan.

2.1.1 **Curriculum decision-making contributes to each child's learning and development outcomes in relation to their identity, connection with community, wellbeing, confidence as learners and effectiveness as communicators.**

As educators, we need to understand the intention behind each experience we offer children and how it impacts on child development and achieves learning outcomes or goals.

2.1.2 **Each child's current knowledge, ideas, culture, abilities and interests are the foundation of the program.**

By using the ideas in the section on discovering children's interests' (page 2) you can design a program that supports their culture, abilities and interests.

3.2.2 **Resources, materials and equipment are sufficient in number, organised in ways that ensure appropriate and effective implementation of the program and allow for multiple uses.**

When setting up experiences it is important that you prepare and provide sufficient resources. This does not mean that you must have 25 of everything – it means that you need to be aware of what your goal is with the experience and who you think will participate, and that you have enough for children to share. Sharing, negotiating, turn-taking and accepting disappointment are also skills we need to support children in acquiring.

3.3.1 Sustainable practices are embedded in service operations.

Take time to think about your service's sustainability strategy. Do you have a veggie patch? What do you do with the vegetables you grow? Do you use tank water? Do you recycle or compost? Do you use recycled materials? Discuss sustainability with colleagues and work out what strategy you wish to take, but be sure to understand why you are doing what you do, and how to articulate this to your community.

3.3.2 Children are supported to become environmentally responsible and show respect for the environment.

Once you have decided on your sustainability strategy, you need to teach the children to support it. Introducing recycling and composting bins to your room, showing children how to put scraps in the compost and ensuring that you aim to cut down on waste are important lessons for children. As educators, we need to be aware of sustainable practices and how these apply to the experiences we offer.

4.2.2 Educators, coordinators and staff members work collaboratively and affirm, challenge, support and learn from each other to further develop their skills, to improve practice and relationships.

Each educator at your service has skills or interests to be fostered. Creating leadership roles for staff using their skills and talents means that the children at your service reap the benefits from every staff member, not just those teaching them

directly. If someone is interested in gardening, they can become the 'gardener' – consulting with children and staff on what plants to buy for the setting, coaching others on gardening skills, and providing resources to support the gardening goals throughout the service. A staff member interested in music might compile a CD for other staff to use that incorporated everyone's favourite songs or the most used music. Staff can nominate their own leadership role, but the benefit is that everyone is respected and valued for what they bring to the program. Working together like this helps all staff acquire new skills, which improves practice and creates a higher quality service for children.

4.2.3 Interactions convey mutual respect, equity and recognition of each other's strengths and skills.

Engaging in team-building experiences such as shared meals out, mentoring one another while developing new skills and celebrating achievements are all ways of reaching this standard. Encouraging staff to work together on shared projects helps them to develop relationships and respect for one another.

5.1 Respectful and equitable relationships are developed and maintained with each child.

5.1.1 Interactions with each child are warm, responsive and build trusting relationships.

5.1.2 Every child is able to engage with educators in meaningful, open interactions that support the acquisition of skills for life and learning.

5.1.3 Each child is supported to feel secure, confident and included.

5.2.1 Each child is supported to work with, learn from and help others through collaborative learning opportunities.

The children in your care rely on you to support them, guide them, care for them and to find qualities in them that you respect and admire. It is our job to ensure we work on developing relationships with *all* children in our care. We need to understand each child deeply so that we can evaluate their actions and respond to those actions appropriately. Sometimes we have to work harder with certain children to find a quality we can nurture, support and extend. However, we have a responsibility to make sure that we do. How can we get to know each child? How can we understand what each child needs? We need to take the time to get to know each child and discover their strengths so we can help them to learn and grow.

6.1.2 Families have opportunities to be involved in the service and contribute to service decisions.

In order to know each child well and support their families in raising their children, we need to find ways of engaging parents in the decisions we are making about their children. Support families to write goals for their children at the beginning of each year, then review these goals mid-year to ensure everyone is working towards meeting these. Provide families with copies of learning stories and invite them to comment on their child's learning before these are put into their portfolio.

Put a 'family contribution' sheet near your sign-in book inviting parents to share ideas of things their children are interested in. Use the skills of parents when developing your program plan. Form parent committees to help create events and assist in managing the service. Invite parents to stay and play so they can see the program you offer and become involved in their child's learning.

As you can see, these quality areas are designed to make sure that children, families and staff are supported to provide and receive the highest quality outcomes. Make sure you understand how these relate to the experiences you are offering to children and practise explaining them in your own words so you can be articulate about the educational programs you are providing.

Chapter 3

The EYLF and learning outcomes

The five learning outcomes defined in *Being, Belonging & Becoming: The Early Years Learning Framework for Australia* (EYLF) provide educators with goals for learning and development. Every play experience you create for children will be supported by one or more of the learning outcomes described in the EYLF.

Many educators will now be adept at understanding which outcomes are most observable in the experiences they create. However, if you are a new graduate or the EYLF is new to you, we encourage you to have a go, refer to the outcomes and evidence of learning listed below and select the few that you feel best reflect the goals of the experience you have designed.

It is also worth noting that the examples of evidence listed under each outcome are just that – examples. The children in your care will demonstrate learning within and across the outcomes in many other ways that that are specific to each children and their family and community, and which will be reflected in the experiences and activities you provide in your setting.

Learning outcome 1: Identity

This outcome strives to support children as they learn about themselves in relation to their family and the community. The relationships each child develops and the experiences they have help to shape their developing identity. If children have positive experiences, whereby they are respected, accepted for who they are and feel safe and secure, they will develop a strong sense of identity.

Feeling safe, secure and supported

This component of LO1 is supported if you observe that children, for example:

- build secure attachment with one and then more familiar educators
- use effective routines to help make predicted transitions smoothly
- sense and respond to a feeling of belonging
- communicate their needs for comfort and assistance

- establish and maintain respectful, trusting relationships with other children and educators
- initiate interactions and conversations
- openly express their feelings and ideas with others
- respond to ideas and suggestions from others
- explore and engage with social and physical environments through relationships and play
- initiate and join in play
- explore aspects of identity through role play

Developing their emerging autonomy, interdependence, resilience and sense of agency

This component of LO1 is supported if you observe that children, for example:

- demonstrate awareness of the needs and rights of others
- are open to new challenges, make new discoveries
- increasingly cooperate and work collaboratively with others
- take considered risks and cope with the unexpected
- recognise their own achievements and the achievements of others
- demonstrate an increasing capacity for self-regulation
- approach new safe situations with confidence
- begin to initiate negotiating and sharing behaviours

- persist when face with challenges and when first attempts are not successful

Developing knowledge and confident self-identities

This component of LO1 is supported if you observe that children, for example:

- feel recognised and respected for who they are
- explore different identities and points of view
- share aspects of their culture
- use their home language to construct meaning
- explore other cultures without compromising their own cultural identities
- develop their social and cultural heritage through engagement with all community members
- reach out and communicate for comfort, companionship and assistance
- celebrate their contributions and achievements with others

Learning to interact with others with care, empathy and respect

This component of LO1 is supported if you observe that children, for example:

- show interest in other children and being part of a group
- engage in and contribute to shared play experiences
- express a wide range of emotions, thoughts and views constructively

- empathise with and express concern for others
- display awareness of and respect for others' perspectives
- reflect on their actions and consider consequences for others

Learning outcome 2: Community

This outcome deals with how children build on a positive sense of identity and the respectful, responsive relationships they have experienced to develop their sense of community and become active contributors to their world. Learning experiences should demonstrate understanding and respect for each child's culture and their family's context in order to help them to become caring and supportive members of their community.

Children learn who they are in the early childhood setting, where the setting sits in the community and how the community sits within the world, and they learn that they have rights and some responsibilities in relation to the wider community.

Belonging, rights and responsibilities in civic participation

This component of LO2 is supported if you observe that children, for example:

- recognise that they have the right to belong to many communities
- cooperate with others and negotiate roles in play episodes and group experiences
- take action to assist other children to participate in social groups

- broaden their understanding in the world in which they live
- express an opinion in matters that affect them
- build on their own social experiences to explore other ways of being
- participate in reciprocal relationships
- learn to read the behaviours of others and respond appropriately
- understand different ways of contributing through play and projects
- demonstrate a sense of belonging and comfort in their environments
- are playful and respond positively to others
- contribute to fair decision-making in matters that affect them

Responding to diversity with respect

This component of LO2 is supported if you observe that children, for example:

- begin to show concern for others
- explore the diversity of heritage, background, culture and tradition
- become aware of connections, similarities and differences between people
- listen to others ideas and respect different ways of being and doing
- practice inclusive ways of being to achieve co-existence
- notice and react in positive ways to similarities and differences among people

Becoming aware of fairness

This component of LO2 is supported if you observe that children, for example:

- recognise unfairness and bias and act with compassion and kindness
- explore connections between people
- are empowered to make choices and problem solve to meet their needs
- begin to think critically about fair and unfair behaviour

Becoming socially responsible and showing respect for the environment

This component of LO2 is supported if you observe that children, for example:

- use play to investigate, project and explore new ideas
- participate with others to solve problems and contribute to group outcomes
- demonstrate knowledge and respect for natural and constructed environments

- explore, infer, predict and hypothesise in order to develop an increased understanding of the interdependence between land, people, plants and animals
- explore relationships with other living and non-living things and observe, notice and respond to change and the impact of human activity
- develop awareness of the impact of human activity on environments and the interdependence of living things

Learning outcome 3: Wellbeing

This learning outcome focuses on the physical and psychological wellbeing of each child. Developing confidence, enjoying happiness and satisfaction and learning to take care of ourselves during challenging times are all important in teaching children to be responsible for their health and wellbeing.

Becoming strong in social and emotional wellbeing

This component of LO3 is supported if you observe that children, for example:

- demonstrate trust and confidence
- are there for others at times of distress, confusion and frustration
- share humour, happiness and satisfaction
- seek out and accept new challenges and make new discoveries
- celebrate their own and others' efforts and achievements
- increasingly cooperate and work with others
- enjoy moments of solitude
- recognise individual achievement and show independence
- make choices and take considered risks
- manage change and cope with frustrations and the unexpected
- understand, self-regulate and manage their own emotions
- acknowledge and accept affirmation
- assert capabilities and independence while demonstrating increasing awareness of the needs and rights of others
- recognise contributions to shared projects and experiences

13

Taking responsibility for health and physical wellbeing

This component of LO3 is supported if you observe that children, for example:

- recognise and communicate their bodily needs
- are happy, healthy, safe and connected to others
- combine gross and fine motor skills and balance in movement activities
- explores the world using their sensory capabilities
- move around their environment confidently and safely demonstrating spatial awareness
- manipulate equipment with increasing competence and skill
- share cultures via movement, storytelling, music and dance
- show awareness of healthy lifestyle and good nutrition
- show competence in personal hygiene, care and safety for themselves and others
- show enthusiasm for physical play and are aware of the safety and wellbeing of themselves and others

Learning outcome 4: Learning

With this learning outcome, educators are encouraging children to explore the world, ask questions, try new things, take considered risks and become inquisitive. Developing creativity, curiosity, enthusiasm and persistence during challenging times are important for developing a love of learning. The ability to problem solve, experiment, research and investigate are vital skills for learning more about the world.

Developing dispositions for learning

This component of LO4 is supported if you observe that children, for example:

- express wonder and interest in their environment
- are curious and active participants in their learning
- use play to investigate, imagine, explore ideas and be creative
- follow and extend their own interests with enthusiasm, energy and concentration
- initiate and contribute to play experiences emerging from their own ideas
- participate in a variety of rich and meaningful inquiry-based activities
- persevere and experience the satisfaction of achievement
- persist even when they find a task difficult

Developing a range of skills and processes

This component of LO4 is supported if you observe that children, for example:

- apply thinking strategies and solve problems in new situations
- create and use representation to organise, record and communicate mathematical ideas and concepts
- make predictions and generalisations about their daily activities, aspects of the natural world and environments

- develop the ability to mirror, repeat and practise actions of others, now or later
- make connections between experiences, concepts and processes
- use play, reflection and investigation to solve problems
- apply generalisations from one situation to a new context
- try out strategies that were effective to solve problems in one situation in a new context
- transfer knowledge from one setting to another

- use patterns they generate or identify and communicate these using mathematical language and symbols
- explore their environment
- follow areas of interest through research and investigation
- manipulate objects and experiment with cause and effect, trial and error
- contribute constructively to mathematical discussions and arguments
- use reflective thinking to consider why things happen and what can be learnt from these experiences

Connecting with people, place, technologies and materials

This component of LO4 is supported if you observe that children, for example:

- engage in learning relationships
- use their senses to explore natural and built environments
- experience the benefits and pleasures of shared learning exploration
- use resources such as tools, media, sounds and graphics
- investigate, take apart, assemble, invent and construct manipulative resources
- use information technology to investigate and solve problems
- explore ideas and theories using imagination, creativity and play
- use feedback to revise and build on an idea

Transferring and adapting learning

This component of LO4 is supported if you observe that children, for example:

- engage with and co-construct learning

Learning outcome 5: Communication

Children need to be able to communicate their needs and understand others in order to connect with the community and be part of their world.

The foundations for developing competencies in literacy and numeracy, so essential for children's successful learning, are laid through a range of learning experiences in early childhood. These experiences should build on those that children have within their families and communities.

- use Standard Australian English and home language to communicate and meet the listener's needs
- interact with others to explore ideas and concepts, clarify and challenge thinking, negotiate and share new understandings
- convey and construct messages with purpose and confidence
- exchange ideas, feelings and understandings using language in play
- demonstrate an understanding of measurement and number, using appropriate vocabulary to describe size, length, volume, capacity and number names
- express ideas and feelings and respect the perspectives of others
- use language to communicate thinking about quantities to describe attributes of objects and collections, and explain mathematical ideas

Interacting verbally and non-verbally with others

This component of LO5 is supported if you observe that children, for example:

- engage in enjoyable interactions using verbal and non-verbal language
- convey and construct messages with purpose and confidence
- build on family and community literacies
- respond verbally and non-verbally to what they see, hear, touch, smell and taste
- use language and representations from play, music and art to share and project meaning
- contribute ideas and experiences in play and group discussions
- attend and give cultural clues that they are listening to and understanding what is said to them

Engaging with text

This component of LO5 is supported if you observe that children, for example:

- listen and respond to speech, stories and rhymes in context
- interact with a range of texts and respond appropriately
- sing and chant rhymes, jingles and songs
- use literacy and numeracy in role play
- begin to understand key literacy concepts such as the sounds of language, letter–sound relationships and concepts of print
- actively use and enjoy language and texts in a range of ways

Expressing ideas and using a range of media

This component of LO5 is supported if you observe that children, for example:

- use language and play to imagine and create roles, scripts and ideas
- share the stories of their own culture and re-enact well-known stories
- use creative arts such as drawing, painting, sculpture, drama, dance, movement, music and storytelling to express ideas and make meaning
- try new ways of expressing ideas and meaning using a range of media
- begin to use images, and approximations of letters and words to convey meaning

Understanding symbols and pattern systems

This component of LO5 is supported if you observe that children, for example:

- use symbols in play to represent and make meaning
- begin to make connections to feelings, ideas, words and actions and those of others
- notice and predict regular routines and the passing of time
- begin to be aware of the relationships between oral, written and visual representations
- develop an understanding that symbols are a powerful means of communication and that ideas, thoughts and concepts can be represented through them
- listen to and respond to sounds and patterns in speech, stories and rhyme

- begin to sort, categorise, order and compare collections and events and attributes of objects and materials
- draw on memory to complete a task
- draw on their experiences in constructing meaning using symbols

Using information and communication technologies

This component of LO5 is supported if you observe that children, for example:

- identify the uses of technologies in everyday life and use it in their play
- use information and communication technologies to access information and images, explore perspectives and make sense of their world
- use information and communication technologies as tools for designing, drawing, editing, reflecting and composing
- engage with technology for fun and to make meaning

In Summary

The standards and elements from the NQS, together with the learning outcomes from the EYLF, provide educators with guidelines for planning quality programs for young children. Educators need to become sufficiently comfortable with these frameworks to be able to use them to describe the intention for their planning. Knowledge, and the ability to articulate that knowledge, are the keys to developing a deeper understanding of why we do what we do. Once you can articulate your intention, you can help others to understand the importance of the plans you create.

Chapter 4

The ocean

The beach ~ Sea life ~ Polar seas ~ Pirates and mermaids ~ Lighthouses

Spending warm summer days jumping through waves, checking out rock pools, collecting shells and building sand castles are just a few of the magical activities to be enjoyed at the beach.

The beach is a wonderful place for children to make new discoveries and investigate, and to be inquisitive and curious about ocean life. This area of interest also provides a great opportunity to discuss the importance of sustainability and caring for our environment.

Ocean life can be explored throughout every play area in your setting. There are creative art and craft experiences, ideas for role play, play dough, drawing and construction, plus wonderful project ideas, incorporating IT and literacy experiences.

In this chapter we share some ideas of things you could do in your service to enhance the children's creativity, imagination and learning opportunities. Use these ideas as a guide. There will be many ways of extending the experiences or adjusting them to suit the context of the group of children you teach. Refer to chapters 2 and 3 to see how you can support this interest area.

Open-ended experiences

This open-ended experience is set up in a tub with water, adding another dynamic to the space. The blue table cover and gemstone colours complement each other, making the experience visually appealing and enabling the children to explore their senses and make new discoveries.

This sensory experience encourages children to imagine and create as they explore their senses and manipulate the arctic animals. We used small foam packaging balls and artificial snow to create a 'snow' sensory tub.

Manipulative play spaces

The felt pirates and mermaids not only look great but they also feel lovely and soft. This experience has been set up with a little treasure chest and gold coins to extend the children's learning and imagination. The experience encourages the children to role play and interact with one another.

'Icicle gemstones' like these can be found in discount shops. We made igloos from white play dough and used laminated dollies as placemats to define each individual work space. This experience enables the children to role play while they talk about polar life.

This experience has been set up for one child on a small table. Creating these little 'nook' play spaces enables the child to enjoy times of solitude. It's a relaxing place to have some quiet time exploring and rearranging the materials as they please. The small amount of coloured water is also inviting and appealing to the senses.

For this experience we used shells coloured with food dye and play dough shaped into a bowl and filled with sand. This experience extends the children's learning and may provide discussions about the ocean and marine life, thus broadening their understanding of the world in which we live.

Adding beach umbrellas and glitter makes this play dough experience inviting, and encourages the children to explore their senses and develop social interactions.

Painting experiences

In this experience we set up the iPad screen at the easel and played a slideshow of tropical fish so the children could see the many different colours and patterns of the fish, and seek to reinvent them through their painting.

Paper towel or coffee filter paper is wonderful for using primary-coloured food dye with pipette droppers. Use the droppers to drop small amounts of dye onto the paper, which quickly absorbs the dye. When two colours combine, children can explore colour mixing and the wonder of discovering new colours. Once the towel is dried you can cut it out into sea creature shapes to add to a sea theme display.

Painted hand prints are an easy way to create bodies for sea creatures. Here we have examples of handprint jellyfish. This not only supports children's developing sensory skills, but it provides the opportunity to extend their knowledge of sea creatures.

Talking with the children about the shapes and features of various sea creatures supports them to take on new challenges and attempt to paint complex shapes.

Drawing experiences

Setting up the drawing table with sea life figurines in a tank provides the children with a more inviting stimulus to draw. In discussions with the children, it is helpful to break the shapes down before they begin drawing. For example, a fish simply broken down is an oval and a triangle.

Craft experiences

In this experience the children are using polystyrene trays to create turtles. Having a sample enables children to see the finished product and encourages them to think about the next step in their creation. These sea turtles were a great challenge for the children to practise cutting. They cut out a template of the turtle's head, flippers and tail.

Here the children are using sea-star shapes cut out of coloured card. They have been provided with squares of tissue that they scrunch into little balls thus supporting their fine motor development. This experience supports the development of the pincer grip.

You can create seaweed using food-dyed pasta, fruit loops and strips of green and blue paper. Threading assists fine motor development and the ability to make choices. (When using food in children's play spaces, consider the philosophy of your centre as well as the cultural and socio-economic circumstances of the families.)

Children created jellyfish using bowls, cellophane, crepe paper, streamers and ribbons. We started by dying the bowls using edicol dyes and droppers. Then we added the tentacles using the various craft materials. This two-staged art experience helps the children to develop the skills and knowledge required for taking on projects.

Sensory experiences

In an ice sensory experience you can freeze plastic sea creatures from your resource cupboard, and add glitter or food dye to enhance the visual effect. The children love to watch the ice melt, and learn more about freezing and melting.

Water beads are a lovely way for children to explore their sensory capabilities. This experience offers children who are resistant to sensory experiences the opportunity to explore without getting too messy. You can purchase these at art and craft stores or online.

Group projects

Working on group projects helps extend children's current interest and celebrates individual children's contributions to sharing their thoughts and ideas. A small idea can be steered into many weeks' worth of interest and learning. Such projects allow all children to contribute to the experience, and to feel a sense of achievement and belonging to a group.

This 2-metre long wire and papier mache whale was created after a group discussion about whales. The children's interest was sparked in a discussion about a whale's size. They were encouraged to think of how we could create a whale on a large scale.

First we shared pictures of whales on our IT screen. We then gave the children clipboards to try to recreate the shape we would need to make a whale. After looking through the children's drawing 'plans' we decided the whale needed to be 'big and round'. We achieved the shape by wrapping chicken wire around a large bucket and manipulating the rest of the wire into the body shape. We added the fin, flippers and tail using chicken wire also. The children used squares of cut-up newspaper and a mixture of papier mache glue to cover the frame.

Once we had the whole frame covered with a thick layer of papier mache, the children painted the whale. This kind of structure can be done on a smaller scale using the same materials.

Books to read

Rainbow Fish by Marcus Pfister
There's a Sea in My Bedroom by Margaret Wild
I Wish I Had a Pirate Suit by Pamela Allan
The Whale's Song by Dyan Sheldon
Mr McGee and the Sea by Pamela Allen
Commotion in the Ocean by Giles Andreae
Mr Seahorse and *A House for Hermit Crab* by Eric Carle
Looking for Crabs by Bruce Whatley
Greetings from Sandy Beach by Bob Graham
Grandpa and Thomas by Pamela Allan
The Lighthouse Keeper's Lunch by Ronda Armitage
Magic Beach by Alison Lester
Tough Borris by Mem Fox
The Snail and the Whale by Julia Donaldson

Dramatic play

Creating rock pools and water areas inside your room can provide opportunities for children to role play and explore. A shell pool or a water trough, with or without water, provides the perfect space for the ocean creatures, shells, rocks and even some ice cubes to extend the play. The hanging streamers add to the atmosphere.

Murals

There are so many aspects of the ocean to explore, and a great way to display some of the learning and creativity going on is by making a mural. As a backdrop you could use blue paints sponged onto a large piece of paper or, as alternative, you might like to use blue cellophane on a window (as pictured above). Incorporating paper rocks, seaweed, coral and netting really makes the ocean come to life.

IT activities

There is some great video footage online to extend children's interest. Showing sea turtles laying eggs, watching fish swim through a coral reef, watching a whale breach out of the water, seeing dolphins swim and jump, watching how sea horses dance through the water are all beautiful things to see and discuss. Images of ocean creature can be used near the easel to stimulate children's creativity.

Community engagement

As part of your goal for developing socially responsible children, you could discuss how rubbish and pollution affect marine life and its environment. This supports the acquisitions of knowledge and skills in relation to quality area 3 and developing children's awareness of sustainability

Reflection questions for group time

- What things can you find at the beach?
- How do fish breathe?
- How do crabs move?
- What colour is seaweed?
- Do fish sleep?
- Do whales have teeth?
- How deep is the ocean?

Chapter 5 — Space

Solar System ~ Aliens ~ Rockets ~ Shuttles
~ Galaxies ~ Moon ~ Stars ~ Astronauts

Dreams of becoming an astronaut, travelling into outer space to discover faraway planets or alien life and walking on the moon all start in early childhood. Supporting young children's interest in space is a veritable wonderland of sensational art and craft, informative discussions, amazing discoveries and a place to let your imagination and creativity run wild.

In this chapter we share some ideas of things you could do to enhance children's creativity, imagination and learning opportunities. Use these ideas as a guide and see if you can think of ways to extend the experiences or adjust them to suit the context of the group of children you teach. Refer to chapters 2 and 3 to see how you can support this interest area.

Open-ended play spaces

Space can be explored throughout every play area in your setting. There are creative art and craft experiences, ideas for role play, play dough, drawing and construction, plus wonderful project ideas, incorporating IT, cooking and literacy experiences.

Open-ended play experiences provide children with opportunity to use their imagination, explore new ideas and regulate their behaviour. This experience was created using dirt, rocks, glow stars, foil patty pans and space vehicles. Placing the red and silver fabric on the table and backing the experience with black card enhances the overall presentation.

There are wonderful timber play sets available for children to explore their interest in space. If you cannot source one, you could create your own using boxes and some spray paint that will provide hours of fun for the space

Manipulative play spaces

This play-dough experience really comes alive with the use of the silver fabric. To protect the fabric, the table is covered with clear plastic or cellophane. The star placemats can be created using a jigsaw or bought from your local hardware or craft supplier, but could also be made from cardboard and laminated. You can make black play dough using black food dye from your local cake supply shop.

A few rocks and space toys with a sprinkle of glitter and you have a delightful, creative and inviting space-inspired play dough experience. Play dough supports children in regulating behaviour due to its relaxing atmosphere, helps develop fine motor skills and encouraged language development.

station enthusiast. Experiences such as this, support children to develop turn-taking skills, problem-solving skills and negotiation tactics.

Kids Knex are a terrific tool for creating crazy outer-space creatures. The wonderful colours and well-designed pieces allow for creativity and autonomy. Manipulating these pieces develops fine motor skills and problem-solving abilities.

By combining 'moon rocks' and black play dough, this experience provides children with opportunities to role play and supports them in developing their identities.

This alien-inspired play dough was introduced after a discussion about space where the children talked about what sorts of creatures might live there. The use of curled-up glitter pipe-cleaners and google eyes helped make our aliens come to life.

Providing the children with a variety of craft materials enables them to use their imagination to create their own ideas. The conversations during this experience really enhanced their language development and social skills.

We invited a local ceramics teacher from a community arts centre to come and do some ceramics with the children. She helped these children create these wonderful rockets. Bringing people in from the community provides greater opportunities for the children to acquire new skills.

Painting experiences

The children were invited to paint their own aliens. Fluorescent paint combined with glitter paints helped create the effect. This could also be done with poska pens and glitter paint or any other medium you may have at your service. Experiences such as this allow children to develop creativity and self-expression.

Using straws and edicol dyes, the children blew crazy aliens to life. This experience is better for older children as the blowing is hard to do, but a great way to challenge and extend them. It develops motor coordination, self-regulation and taking considered risks.

Recycled construction or deconstruction

Children can dismantle or pull apart old computers and stereos collected from your local recycling centre to create robots and other space junk. The experience of using the screw drivers is wonderful for coordination, fine motor development and concentration, while also providing opportunities for discussion and inquiry.

Connecting an old computer screen to a laptop and placing it at the easel provides visual stimulus and inspiration for the children. You will be amazed at the creativity that comes from this. Gather a series of images from the internet and put these on a USB in the laptop, then run them as a slideshow.

Salad spinner paintings are lots of fun and help children explore cause and effect. You place a paper plate in the salad spinner then some blobs of paint and make it spin. The paint spreads across the plate, creating a great effect.

Once the electrical items are in pieces, the bits can be gathered up and used to make robots and aliens.

This child is creating his solar system using soft pastels. He created this by studying a poster and working out the relative size of each planet and the colours he would use for each. He then stuck the names of each planet with the correct planet. Such activities help children to develop a love of learning.

The exploration of space is a great time to use recycled materials in your art. A visit to your local recycling centre will provide you with mountains of resources to create some really wonderful things. This helps children develop an understanding of sustainability, recycling and taking care of the environment.

Group projects

The solar system

Discussions of space will often lead to the solar system. It is important to try to share facts that support children's learning and to create a solar system that reflects those facts. Using the internet or posters available from educational suppliers, you can learn about which planets are hot or cold, what colour the planets are and why, the relative size of each planet and the correct order of the planets from the sun.

Others ways to create the solar system include using a variety of balls of differing sizes. Decorating these balls with fabric and paper provides opportunities to discuss the features of the planet: *Is there water on this planet? Is it a hot planet? Why is there rust on this planet?*

Engaging in this experience allows children the opportunities to transfer from one setting to another and making decisions about which colours to use on each planet based on previous discussions.

Murals

Creating a space mural can be a lovely, open-ended, creative and free experience. Here the children have painted a black background then painted or stuck on craft items that represent space to them.

RED GROUP

'Alien Attack'

In this experience, they each drew an alien onto a canvas sheet. These were then cut out and glued onto a pre-painted canvas. Canvases are a great way to raise funds for your service. This helps develop an understanding of community and a sense of belonging. Children also gain an understanding to support everyone in the group to work together towards a shared goal.

Dramatic play

If you have a suitable area in your room you might like to create a 'space corner'. Using a roll of black plastic from the hardware store, you can create a tent-like structure that is totally blacked out. Inserting a 'black light' will ensure that everything white, pale coloured or fluorescent inside this tent is illuminated. Create your own astronaut outfits using white clothes and some silver recycled materials. The children will love these. You can make a super control panel using a big box, painted black with fairy lights poking through the box. Put the fairy lights on a twinkling circuit to give a great effect.

You can use glow paint to create some wonderful art and hang this in the tent and it will glow in the dark. The space tent provides a unique element to dramatic play, whereby children can explore new roles and develop their autonomy, social behaviours and the ability to consider other people's ideas.

An old fridge box makes a great child-sized space shuttle. The children can paint it and make the control panel. Put on the astronaut outfits and you're ready for a trip to space. The children will develop their numeracy skills when they count down ready for take-off.

Using old boxes and items from the local recycle centre, these children were able to create a robot family. Pictured here is the Robot Mummy. Using recycled materials supports the service in taking an active role in caring for its environment.

Craft experiences

These sock puppets are a wonderful experience for older children. Using needle and thread, glitter paint and some craft items such as feathers, goggle eyes and pipe-cleaners, the children created their own sock alien. This experience is quite complex and will develop fine motor skills, concentration and coordination.

These robot pastings enable children to make choices and develop creativity and autonomy. Each child chooses which items they will use to design their robot. This supports children acquire a sense of agency, enabling them to make choices and decisions and influence events and their world.

Sensory experiences

This sensory experience supports the children in developing fine motor skills while providing them with the opportunity to explore their senses.

Drawing experiences

Using poska pens on black card, children are able to create quite a unique and brightly colourful drawing. Poska pens lend themselves nicely to space drawings, and the effect of them on black gives the look of outer space.

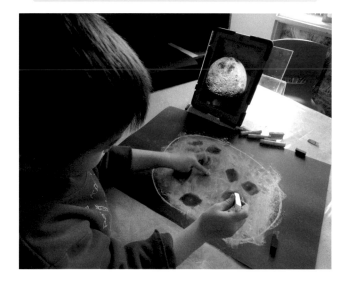

Using soft pastels, these children have made drawings exploring the surface of the moon. They looked at pictures of the moon, talked about colours or shades, and craters and the texture of the moon. They were then inspired to try to draw this themselves. Using the soft pastels they were able to practise a rubbing or smudging effect.

Using the same technique described above, the children looked at pictures of the sun. We talked about it being a ball of fire and how we could see the fire shooting of the sun. We talked about the heat coming off the sun and about how we can feel that down here on earth.

If you stick squares of aluminium foil on the card first, it provides a different experience altogether. Drawing is a relaxing experience, enabling the children to regulate their behaviour and encouraging them to openly express their ideas with others.

Children drew space drawings using a combination of oil pastels and then combined those with painting. By mixing the mediums, children can create texture on their art work. Children can use this medium to investigate, imagine, explore ideas and be creative.

Using fine black fine liners helps children to include more detail in their drawings. The focus is more on the actual drawing than on colour, so they tend to include more detail. This helps children to make new discoveries, cooperate with others, develop fine motor skills and enjoy moments of solitude.

Cooking experiences

Some fun ideas for cooking that relate to an exploration through space might include: making salt dough and then turning it into rockets, aliens or planets, or making veggie monsters using a variety of vegetable brought in by the children. These not only promote healthy eating but also encourage children to try new things. They take their veggie monster home that night and eat it with their family.

IT activities

Use Google Earth to look at pictures of the earth taken from satellites. Apps such as Night Sky allow you to hold the iPad up and see where the planets and constellations are. This will support learning and extend exploration of outer space. Children will have the opportunity to engage with technology, identify uses within everyday life and learn that they can access information to assist learning.

Books to read

Aliens in Underpants and *Aliens in Underpants Save the World* by Claire Freedman

Twinkle by Nick Bland

Roaring Rockets by Tony Mitton

Max goes to Mars, *Space: A Visual Encyclopaedia* and *Zoom Rocket Zoom* by Margret Mayo

How to Catch a Star by Oliver Jeffers

Goodnight Moon by Margaret Wise Brown

Community engagement

A visit to the planetarium will enable older children to thoroughly investigate space and the planets. At your local science museum (such as Scienceworks in Melbourne or Questacon in Canberra) there are many activities and opportunities for learning available to children.

Engaging within the community empowers children to make choices and problem solve, explore, infer, predict and hypothesise to develop an increased understanding of the world in which they live.

This display of children's artwork and the annual show demonstrates that we respect the contributions children make to the community.

Reflection questions for group time

- What is space?
- What is a star?
- Are aliens real?
- How do rockets work?
- What are the planets?
- Can we visit space?
- Who travels to outer space?
- Is earth a planet?
- How big is earth (in comparison to other planets)?

Chapter 6

Dinosaurs

Fossils ~ Carnivores ~ Herbivores ~ Omnivores ~ Palaeontologists ~ Volcanoes

Dinosaurs are always a favourite with children and this interest can be explored throughout every play area in your setting. In this chapter we share some ideas of what you could do to enhance the children's creativity, imagination and learning opportunities. Use these ideas as a guide and refer to chapters 2 and 3 to see how you can support this interest area

Open-ended play spaces

Using natural pieces such as rocks and logs creates a great space for children to further explore dinosaurs. Discussions about the features of each different type of dinosaur helps extend thinking and learning.

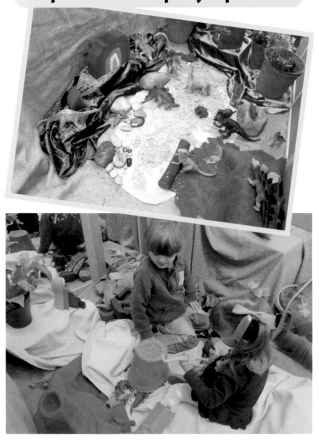

Manipulative play spaces

Clay is a great material for children to explore using their sensory capabilities. It helps to develop fine motor skills and allows them to create with a tactile medium.

These play spaces were created by using hessian as a base then adding blocks, rocks and logs to create many different levels. The use of real foliage, sand and natural colours creates an inviting space for children to imagine, explore and be creative.

Painting experiences

We talked about how there were lots of active volcanoes at the time of the dinosaurs, and how they could have contributed to dinosaur extinction. This painting of a volcano was inspired by a child's interest after a discussion about how volcanos erupt. We talked about the shapes we would need to create the volcano itself and then later added the lava. This can extend into creating volcanoes that actually erupt, using bicarbonate of soda and vinegar (see p. 37).

When children are painting or drawing dinosaurs it is a good idea to stand and talk about the features of the dinosaurs. This helps children develop their creativity and artistic skills and allows them to try new things and take considered risks.

Dramatic play

Making dinosaur puppets and costumes helps the children in role play and developing their identities. These could support group times when singing dinosaur songs or could be used in drama sessions to create dinosaur stories.

Sensory experiences

This fossil dig experience was set up inside a deep tub using kinetic sand or 'moon sand'. You can find this at a craft store or online. Moon sand can be moulded and shaped around dinosaur figurines to create 'fossils' for the children to find and explore using brushes or other tools.

Dinosaur eggs are great for children to explore using small hammers to find the dinosaurs. Using dirt, flour and water you can make a thick paste to cover a plastic dinosaur figurine and place in the oven to bake until hard. The children will enjoy discovering the fossils. You can just see the eggs poking through the dirt, awaiting their discovery.

This striking stegosaurus was created by using black fine liner pen then sticking small cut-up pieces of tissue paper over the top. It is preferable for children to draw their own dinosaur as this supports their creativity. Even children as young as 3 can do this.

Sand pits and dirt patches are a great place to use dinosaur figurines. These spaces allow children to explore their natural environment using their sensory capabilities. These experiences support the career goals of your budding palaeontologists.

A display of dinosaur figurines helps children to understand the shapes needed to create the unique features of each dinosaur. If they were drawing a stegosaurus you could talk about the plates along their back, their short legs and their small head.

Using these descriptive words while the child is drawing helps to break the dinosaur down into more manageable steps

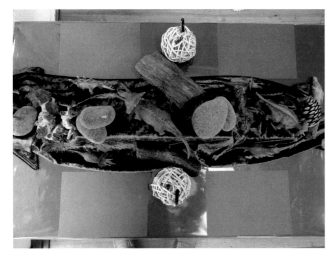

This drawing table help expand the child's thinking and imagination, the inviting set up of the tables aid creativity and exploration.

Craft experiences

Rock dinosaurs were created using small rock and pebbles and gluing them down onto a piece of thick card. The children decided which dinosaur shape they would like to make then designed their dinosaur by arranging the rocks onto the card. An adult then used a glue gun to glue the rock pieces in place.

These box construction dinosaurs were firstly put together using card board rolls, boxes and sticky tape. Once the body was assembled the children painted the dinosaurs on a separate table, using the colours they thought best suited the type of dinosaur they created.

Group projects

Creating a volcano is a great group experience. Start by building up some sand into a 'volcano' shape in your sand pit or a large container. Once it is high enough, make a hole in the top and insert a thin plastic cup or cardboard tube. Inside the tube place bicarbonate of soda and red food dye or powder paint to create 'red lava'. You can then make your volcano erupt by pouring vinegar into the tube. This experience supports the children's learning, scientific discoveries and allows multiple opportunities for discussion.

Murals

This dinosaur mural was created by painting on a large piece of paper roll.

We started by painting the background then later added dinosaurs which were inspired by the children's drawings. These were transferred on to the mural using the overhead projector to enlarge their drawings.

Community engagement

A visit to the museum to view dinosaur bones and fossils will give the children a better understanding of the size and shapes dinosaurs were. In some areas of Australia there may be drama groups that can visit your service and extend the children's learning, confidence and interest.

Books to read

Saturday Night at the Dinosaur Stomp by Carole Diggory

Dinosaur ROAR! by Paul & Henrietta Stickland

Harry and His Bucket Full of Dinosaurs by Ian Whybrow & Adrian Reynolds

How Do Dinosaurs Say I Love You? by Jane Yolen (there is a series by this author How do Dinosaurs ...?)

If The Dinosaurs Came Back by Bernard Most

Dinosaur Time by Michael Foreman

Reflection questions for group time

- What are fossils?
- What kinds of dinosaurs were there? What did they look like?
- What did dinosaurs eat?
- What is a volcano?
- How big were dinosaurs?
- Are there still dinosaurs around today?
- What does a palaeontologist do?

Chapter 7

Gardens and minibeasts

Bugs ~ Beetles ~ Spiders ~ Sustainability ~ Veggie patch ~ Snails ~ Butterflies

Gardens provide endless opportunities for children to investigate living things. Every garden allows children to create, explore, imagine, run free, and make numerous discoveries. There is something in the garden for everyone.

There are many opportunities throughout your service to offer children experiences that relate to garden and insects. Bringing the outdoors inside is a wonderful way for them to explore in a different setting such as bringing a digging patch inside (see photo above). These explorations also help to develop children's awareness that we can grow fruit and vegetables in gardens and to learn about how this take place.

In this chapter we look at many ideas that you can introduce and implement in your service. Suggestions include: setting up an insect digging patch in your room, drawing insects, observing and painting flowers, minibeasts made from plasticine or play dough, acting out the hungry caterpillar story, observing gardens and insects on the IT screen.

Use these ideas as a guide and see if you can think of ways of extending these experiences or adjusting them to suit the context of the group of children you teach.

Refer to chapters 2 and 3 to see how you can support this interest area

Open-ended play spaces

Providing open-end play spaces enables children to participate in play experiences at their own level. These play spaces provide them with endless opportunities to use their imagination, to create or to play alone when they need a moment's solitude, and to self-regulate their behaviour.

This experience is designed by using a mirror and this creates a 3D effect. We added insects such as beetles, spiders, worms, and butterflies, some natural objects such as pinecones and twigs, and some greenery to enhance the overall presentation.

Here children are using magnifying glasses to look for insects such as ladybirds and other creatures that live 'at the bottom of the garden'.

This snail experience allows the children to bring in their own snails from home. The experience allows the children to observe the snails while they are playing. Discussions in relation to the feature of a snail and their fascinating snail trail helps extend children's learning.

These play experiences were created in response to the children's fascination with fairies. The experience was set up for two or more children which promotes social interaction, and also encourages the children to use their imagination.

Manipulative play experiences

This play dough experience incorporates natural items from the garden, such as ivy leaves. These define the area and provide the children with a visual of where their allocated space is. The small white ceramic plates are from the local bric-a-brac shop and the pompoms, buttons, black dots and sticks are from a local art and craft supplier. The striking red play dough inspires the children to manipulate, imagine and create. We covered the table with brightly coloured paper protected by a plastic sheet.

This insect play dough experience provides children with a range of tools to manipulate, such as garlic crushers, rolling pins and an assortment of beads, plastic tubing, straws and stones. Adding different craft items prompts the children to create their own insects. They are able to have conversations with one another about what insect they are making which then helps with their social, listening and language skills.

Sensory experiences

Each year we take the opportunity to explore our senses in an autumn corner. Using bird nets from the local hardware store, you can cordon off an area in the corner of the room and fill it with leaves. Encourage the children to gather leaves from streets surrounding their homes and bring them in to your setting. The children can play in this area, throwing leaves around and rolling in them with friends.

Painting experiences

The children were able to look at real flowers at our morning mat time. We then had the opportunity to paint flowers at the easel. We placed a gerbera in a vase next to the easel and provided paints that matched the colour of the flower. Having the visual stimulus helps the children in developing their creativity skills.

Children were then able to experience a different art medium using the flowers to paint with instead of paint brushes. They dipped the flowers in paint then gently dabbed them onto a piece white paper. This created a vibrant colour pattern and the children were able to see the shape of the flower on their piece of paper. This experience helps us develop children's understanding of pattern making.

We discussed what we could observe in relation to foreground, middle ground and background as well as the reflections. For this particular experience the children used water colours. However, we also tried the experience using soft pastels.

Recycled construction

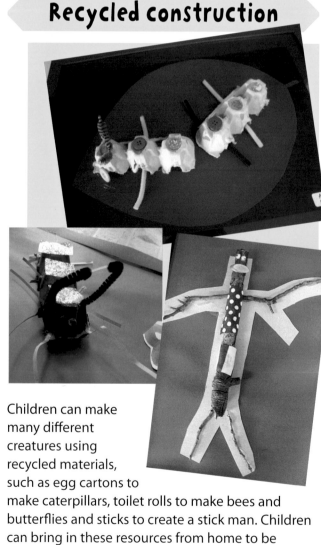

A light table is another way to inspire children. In this instance, children used water colour paints, to recreate the autumn leaves. The light table highlights the leaves as the light shines through them, and the children are able to see the colours and veins of the leaves.

We designed an experience to introduce the children to the painter Claude Monet. First, we used the internet to look images of Monet's garden and the many paintings he made of it, such as *Water Lilies and the Japanese Bridge*.

Children can make many different creatures using recycled materials, such as egg cartons to make caterpillars, toilet rolls to make bees and butterflies and sticks to create a stick man. Children can bring in these resources from home to be shared by the whole group.

Group projects

We have been looking at our garden and talking to the children about other things that we could grow. Some of the children told us that they had a vegetable patch at home. We had a discussion about vegetables and how they are good for us and make us grow strong and keep us healthy. We planted some vegetables with the children's help, and talked about the timeline in relation to the growth of a vegetable. Once it's planted we water it to make it grow, then we pick it and then we cook it to eat.

Then we each made vegie monsters using vegetables brought from home. We looked at and talked about each vegetable and decided which best represented different body parts for our veggie monsters. The children took this home to share with their families that night. The following day we chopped the remaining vegetables up and made fried rice.

Creating a mural can be a lovely way to work together and build on our connections with one another. It makes the children feel valued and a part of a community where we all listen and contribute our ideas. Your mural can be created using paint, or you can add other recycled and craft items to give it texture. The second mural pictured here is our family garden. It contains photos of each child's family.

Dramatic play

It's a lovely idea to create your own digging patch in the room. Using some fake grass turf and an old clam shell you can transform this area into a garden. Place pot plants and logs around the perimeter to create a border for your play space, and add spades, buckets and some fake flowers. You can also create your own rainbow by painting it onto some wood or paper and hanging it up high. This experience helps develop turn-taking and negotiating skills, as well supporting creativity.

Craft experiences

Using recycled foam pieces from our resource rescue centre we created our own caterpillars. The children painted the foam in different colours, and it was used as the body of the caterpillar. We added pipe cleaners to create the legs, and googly eyes to put on the face. This experience helps children with their fine motor skills, and concentration.

After we read the story *Stickman* by Julia Donaldson we created our own stick man by using sticks that the children had collected. We used fabric to dress our stick man. Incorporating nature into the craft experience broadens the children's understating of using items from our natural environment.

Drawing experiences

An ideal way to explore snails brought in by the children is to draw them. Using an old fish tank, filled with some rocks, leaves and a log, covered with a net so that the snails could breathe but not escape at the same time, is a great way to contain our garden friends. Add some magnifying glasses so children to see the snails up close and observe what they are doing before they draw them using black markers.

In this experience, the children are using soft pastels to create these beautiful bees. The combined technique of drawing and smudging creates a great effect.

When setting up a drawing experience it's a good idea to provide some props so that children have a visual prompt. This makes the experience bright and inviting. You can also provide different drawing materials such as oil pastels as above, textas, pencils, charcoal and soft. Soft pastels have a vibrant colour, and once the drawing is complete children can use their fingers to create a smudged look.

Sensory experiences

We also explored the use of leaves. If leaves are placed underneath the paper the children can gently rub their crayon over the paper and slowly the leaf will appear.

These experiences provide an opportunity for the children to use their senses, to explore, discover, use their imagination and apply their creative thinking. The purple lavender rice is a calming experience as children are able to smell the lavender. The pink rice experience has been set up to extend the children's interest in fairies.

This sensory tub was set up in response to the children's interest in the book *The Very Hungry Caterpillar*. Using coloured rice and props that represent the book, the children are able to explore the story line through this sensory experience.

Using IT

Children can see all types of minibeasts up close by using images from the internet. This will support them to develop detail in their art and increasing their power of observation.

Community engagement

A visit to a children's garden is always a lovely way for children to get in touch with nature. They can to investigate, explore, and to get their hands dirty, using their senses to explore and to develop an increased understanding of our natural habitat.

Books to read

The Very Hungry Caterpillar by Eric Carle
Princess Chamomile's Garden by Hiawyn Oram
The Bad Tempered Ladybird by Eric Carle
Thirsty Flowers by Toni Wilson
The Very Quiet Cricket by Eric Carle
The Tiny Seed by Eric Carle
The Little House by Virginia Lee Burton
Lily's Garden by Deborah Kogan Ray
How a Seed Grows by Helene Jordan

Reflection questions for group time

- What is an insect?
- What makes flowers grow?
- Do insects all look the same?
- How many legs does an insect have?
- What do insects eat?
- What do bees make?
- What is the role of the queen bee?

Chapter 8

Farms

Cows ~ hens ~ sheep ~ horses ~ farmers ~ crops ~ machinery

The farm provides children with many opportunities to learn about animals and get close to nature. Farms enable children to have hands-on experiences and learn about the different animals that live on a farm. This can lead onto many informative discussions with the children and make some new discoveries and broaden their understanding of other living creatures.

There are many areas in your setting where a farm can be introduced. You can incorporate imaginary play spaces as well as craft and drawing activities, tapping into your local community. Perhaps you could organise a mobile farm to come to setting or plan a journey to a local farm to feed and observe the animals.

Use these ideas as a guide and see if you can think of ways of extending or adjusting the experiences to suit the context of the group of children you teach. Refer to chapters 2 and 3 to see how you can support this interest area.

Open-ended play spaces

Open-ended play spaces provide opportunities for children to create, improvise and explore, enhancing their imagination and their social and emotionally abilities.

This experience has been created by using a round plastic tub and dirt so children can explore their senses by using their hands. We have placed pigs in the dirt, twigs and a dish which is improvised as a trough for the pigs. Children talked about how pigs love rolling around in the mud.

The green mat in this farm experience was made by dying green fabric. We made a blue stream and placed blue gemstones along it to create a sparkle effect. Some greenery has been added and we used an old wooden barn as the farm house. You could also use a crate or a box. While playing in this experience, children naturally communicated with one another, and engaged in turn-taking and cooperation.

For a different experience, we covered a table in some old hessian and created a mini farm using wooden animals, fences, wooden bowls, some natural items such as pine cones and small logs, and some gemstones. We bought the dish from our local op shop and it makes a wonderful pond for ducks. We also added some hay to provide a link to what children would see on real farms. This experience is set up as an inviting play space for one or two children at most and enables them to imagine that they are on a farm.

This is another play space that incorporates wooden farm animals. We used green fabric over the table to symbolise the grass and added fences, moss trees and two wooden boxes to act as farm houses.

Manipulative play spaces

This play dough experience encourages children to use their senses and role-play at the same time. We placed some farm trucks on the table and picked some greenery from our garden to make the farm more natural. The wooden round mats create a rustic feel. You could source small pieces of wood to create the same look. This experience enhances fine motor skills, creativity and imagination, and can also sooth and be calming.

The chicken play dough can be incorporated into your program and will tie in nicely in your setting if you have chicks. The children learnt about the life cycle of a chicken and then observed them in their egg form before they hatched into chickens. You can add materials to this table such as pipe cleaners, googly eyes, feathers, sticks for the beak and a piece of moss grass to create a farm look. Adding materials such as this for the children to use extends the activity as they are able to use their imagination.

Painting experiences

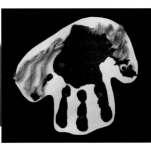

These pictures of a sheep and horse were created using a child's handprint. We painted the children's hands and carefully pressed them onto a piece of paper. Once the handprint was dry, the children decorated their sheep using wool from the local children's farm, and we added some eyes. For the horse's mane and tail we used coarse twine. This experience enables the children to explore their senses and use different textures to create a painting.

Construction

We set up a sponge painting activity so children could create their own farm animal using a different art medium. They first drew a farm animal using a black marker, then gently placed their sponge in the paint and dabbed it on their picture, adding vibrancy and texture. They used their creativity and made choices about the animal they wish to create. Once they completed the sponging experience, we added torn tissue paper to make sky, grass, trees and sunshine.

Children used paint brushes on canvas to create this painting. Canvas provides a different texture and shows children that we respect their talents and abilities.

Outside we created a farm enclosure in the sand pit with wooden building blocks. We used plastic farm animals instead of wooden ones as these are more durable when adding water to the sand pit. There was a bowl of water so the animals could go for a swim and some logs to create a rustic atmosphere. Sand is an excellent open-ended activity, enabling the children to explore their senses, and work collaboratively with each other.

Tap Tap is a great way for children to create a picture using shapes. In this activity, they are using farm animal shapes. This is a creative activity which allows the children to practice hand–eye coordination and fine motor skills.

cows, horses, sheep and farmers – then cut them out and stuck them on. Pasting bird seed on to the mural add a sensory element. Group projects help children to develop a sense of belonging.

Sensory play spaces

This sensory experience was created using bird seed, which can be reused for other experiences. Bird seed is also a great resource for pouring and scooping in a large tub.

Group projects

The children created this farm mural as a joint project. We begin by painting the background and then adding the sky and hill. The children used rollers to paint this, and sponges to create the clouds. Each child created a farm picture – chickens,

Dramatic play

Setting up an animal hospital where children can to look after sick animals extends their farm-related play. Add some stuffed animals, white coats, a medical kit, bandages and baskets. This develops imagination, decision-making skills and cooperation. Dramatic play engages children in role play where they are able to learn and grow along the way.

Craft experiences

In this experience, children created a duck from an assortment of collage materials. They cut out round yellow circles to represent the face, used patty pans to create the beak, pipe-cleaners for the legs and then added feathers to their body. This experience is an activity with a specific desired outcome that demonstrates the children's ability to follow instructions, whilst also supporting their creativity and problem-solving skills.

Drawing experiences

One of the children drew this picture of a duck using a black marker. Drawing supports the children's fine motor development and hand–eye coordination, and helps them to make comparisons between shapes, textures and sizes.

In the second drawing, the children used tissue paper to add a different dimension and texture.

Community engagement

You can take the children to the local children's farm, or have a mobile farm visit you. This supports the children in their learning and discovery about animals and sustainability.

Books to read

Old McDonald Had a Farm by Pam Adams
Big Red Barn by Margaret Wise Brown
My Farm by Alison Lester
Giggle Giggle, Quack by Doreen Cronin
Lucky Pigs by Susan Pooker
Farmer Duck by Martin Waddell & Helen Oxenbury
Fergus the Farmyard Dog by Tony Maddox
Farmer Will by Jane Cowen Fletcher
Pigs in the Mud in the Middle of the Rud by Lynn Plourde

Reflection questions for group time

- Who lives on the farm?
- Who takes care of the animals?
- What do the farm animals eat?
- What sorts of animals live on a farm?
- What is shearing?
- What is hay made from?
- What is a crop?

Wild animals

Zoo ~ Jungle ~ Rainforest ~ Reptiles ~

There are many areas where wild animal play can be introduced into your setting. You can incorporate imaginary play spaces and craft and drawing activities, as well as tapping into your local community by going on a journey to a zoo or animal reserve.

Use these ideas as a guide and see if you can think of ways of extending these experiences or adjusting them to suit the context of the group of children you teach. Refer to chapters 2 and 3 to see how you can support this interest area.

Open-ended play spaces

Creating a reptile experience using figurines, logs, plants, pebbles and a variety of items from

your local op shop provides children with the opportunity to explore reptiles. Providing paper on a clipboard nearby encourages children to draw the creatures.

Here is another way to display the reptiles. The use of water adds a sensory element to the experience. Sitting with the children as they play and having discussions about the reptiles can extend their thinking.

In this experience the children are presented with plastic turtles and natural items such as pebbles, stones and rocks, and other items from op shops and the local hardware store. Combined, these enable children to play alone, explore the world around them and regulate their behaviour.

Manipulative play spaces

These play dough experiences combine African animals and play dough with natural leaves and fences. Children can manipulate the play dough while creating their own imaginative play space.

Painting experiences

This lion-head painting was created after first talking to the child about breaking down the shapes. We talked about the face shape (a circle) then what a lions mane looks like (lots of stripy lines around the face). We also discussed the colours we would need to create this look.

We created handprint lions using the handprint as the lion's body. We cut slits around the edges of a patty pan to make a mane, then drew a face in the middle.

For this acrylic on canvas painting the child focused on the details of the body parts first, then added the details such as the stripes and teeth later.

Sensory experiences

Using dirt inside provides children with the opportunity to engage in messy play and explore the animals while chatting with their friends. Bringing the outdoors inside provides opportunities to explore the natural environment in a different setting.

Craft experiences

Children can create box construction animals using small cardboard boxes and sticky tape. Adding ears, tails and trunks or other features helps bring the animal to life. Once the boxes are constructed, the children might like to paint their animal on a different table.

Drawing experiences

These drawings were created using soft pastels. By drawing the shapes first then smudging the drawings with their fingertips, the children were able to achieve a beautiful effect and texture. Engaging in this experience after a visit to the zoo, where the children have had opportunity to see these animals in real life, will make the experience even more meaningful.

You can provide different examples of animal patterns on small square cards for children, so that they can see what makes each pattern unique. They can then reproduce the pattern they have chosen by drawing in black fine liner first then adding coloured pencil.

This beautiful art piece was created by first drawing the elephant with black fine liner pen. The grey tissue paper and sequin diamonds were then added afterwards, and the drawing was cut out and pasted onto coloured card to improve presentation.

Group projects

After the children have drawn an animal onto A4 paper with a black fine line pen, you can copy their drawing onto transparency sheets. You can then project the picture onto a large roll of paper and the children can trace around the enlarged image. These can then be painted and cut out as the final product.

Dramatic play

A wonderful experience for children is re-creating the *Dear Zoo* story by Rod Campbell. Get a large box (shoe box, gift box) as well as several small boxes. Inside each small box place a different zoo animal figurine. Place a puppy figurine in a small box and hide this in your pocket. Place all the other small boxes inside the large box. Start telling the story, allowing a child to choose a box and open it each time. Continue this until you are down to the last box. Once the last box is chosen, quietly slip the puppy box back into the main box. Invite a child to open the last box to reveal the puppy and, just as in the story, the puppy is perfect and we will keep him.

BOOKS TO READ

Dear Zoo by Rod Campbell

The Animal Boogie by Debbie Harter

Giraffes Can't Dance by Giles Andreae

Willy the Wimp by Anthony Brown

Polar Bear, Polar Bear What Do You Hear?
by Bill Martin Jr & Eric Carle

Rumble in the Jungle by Giles Andreae

The Tiger Who Came to Tea by Judith Kerr

Community engagement

A trip to the zoo can provide your service with countless amounts of program and experiences. Taking some art supplies with you such as clip boards, paper and pencils gives your children an opportunity to draw what they see while they are at the zoo.

IT activities

Set up a computer to show a 'live zoo cam' via a zoo website. The children will be able to watch the animals in their enclosures and then draw what they see.

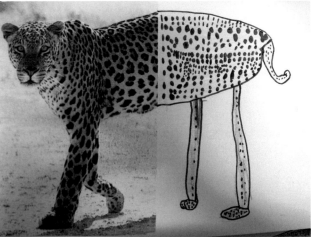

Find images from the internet and display them on to an IT screen. You can also print the pictures off onto A4 paper. Then cut the animals in half and ask the children to draw the other half of what they think is missing. This supports the children's ability to develop the power of observation, listening to instructions and their fine motor skills.

Questions for reflection

- Why do we have zoos?
- What kinds of animals can you see at the zoo?
- What do lions (zebras, giraffes, etc.) eat?
- What does a zoo keeper do?
- Where do gorillas (hippos, snakes, etc.) live?

Chapter 10

Transport and buildings

**Cars ~ Trains ~ Trucks ~ Cities ~ Building ~
Fire trucks ~ Ambulances**

Most children love learning about the different types of vehicles we use. We can help children identify these vehicles and their purposes, by asking questions such as *What do fire engines do? Where would we find a tractor? What sort of vehicles deliver mail? What carries people up in the sky?* and discovering the answers together.

Children love to build – with anything available, and there are suggestions here to extend vocabulary, develop motor skills and encourage collaboration.

Use these ideas as a guide and see if you can think of ways of extending or adjusting the experiences to suit the context of the group of children you teach. Refer to chapters 2 and 3 to see how you can support these interest areas.

Transport can be incorporated into your service in many ways – sandpit, digging patch, painting easels, box construction table, sensory tubs, floor space and play dough. These activities help to extend children's vocabulary, and also provide opportunities for classifying and categorising.

Open-ended play spaces

This play space has been set up in a wooden box with sand, road signs and transport vehicles added. We placed a yellow tablecloth underneath to highlight the yellow vehicles in the sand. The children manipulate the vehicles in the sand and use their imagination and cognitive skills to create roads.

We added a book to create an extension to this experience. Children have access to these books and are able to look at them while they are playing. This helps them to create links between the book and the play experience and gives them a visual prompt. They can also act out the story and use the props provided.

Manipulative play spaces

We provided the children with hats, tools, play dough and wooden building blocks. We used hammers from our tap tap experiences and found some other tools such as a plastic saw, measuring tape and screws. These sets can be picked up from your local toy shop or opportunity shop. The children used their imagination and social skills to role play by being builders.

Painting experiences

Children were invited to observe and paint this fire truck. We provided crayons and water colour paints. The children used the crayons to create the drawing and then they painted over the crayon with the water colours. Water colours are easy to manipulate and provide the drawing with a different texture.

Construction

We set up some Lego mats and a box of Lego pieces at a small table for children to use their imagination and construct items.

Sand and digging patch

Children use their gross motor skills when manoeuvring the trucks in the sandpit. They also have to cooperate with each other and use their spatial awareness.

These boys are creating their own tower. They are carefully placing each block down slowly and are communicating with each about how high they will build and how will they make the tower stay up. They are asking questions, applying thinking strategies and using their fine motor skills to carefully pick up the pieces and place them down.

These children are making 'concrete' by combining sand and water. They are negotiating with each other and working out how much water they need to make concrete and what will be the correct consistency. They apply thinking strategies, listen to one other's suggestions and ideas, and are becoming aware that they belong to a group.

In this experience, the children are making concrete using mud instead of sand, which provides them with another sensory experience. They are experimenting with the consistency and trying to make thick mud so that their wall will stay up, working collaboratively to solve problems.

Sensory experiences

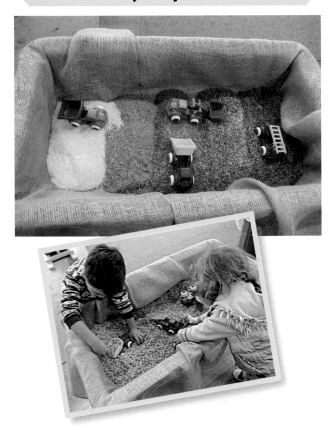

This rainbow sensory rice has been set up for the children to explore colours, and encourages them to manipulate materials such as the trucks and cars. They are also building up their fine motor skills and coordination.

This experience displayed in a wooden tray uses some natural materials along with trucks and cars. Children examine, discover, categorise and make senses of the world through sensory exploration.

Drawing experiences

The children used Texta pens to draw. Drawing with children allows the freedom to express and communicate their ideas and imagination freely.

We placed a fire engine on the table for the children to observe and draw. This experience was set up because we had visited the fire station earlier in the week and the children were able to see fire engines. They linked the activity with a real life experience, transferring their knowledge from one setting to another.

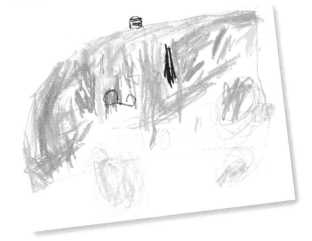

Children enjoy participating in woodwork. These children created their own vehicles using wood, nails and a hammer, painted and decorated them.

Craft experiences

We provided recycled materials such as boxes to encourage children to construct wonderful creations that support their interest.

Group projects

The children showed great interest in creating their own town. We had a town planning meeting to discuss what makes a town. Each child was given a clipboard and took on the role of becoming a town planner. They each contributed their ideas and thoughts which were noted, and then incorporated when we constructed the town as a group. We made roads, buildings, lampposts and signs.

Each child contributed to this project and had the opportunity to express their ideas and thoughts. They were developing their understanding and sense of belonging in the community, and developing their turn-taking skills and ability to listen to each other's ideas.

Dramatic play

The children are having a lovely time being builders and acting out a character. This is an experience where the children can role play and reflect, and is an effective tool as it encourages children to become active participants in their learning.

Reflection questions for group time

- What does an ambulance officer… (police officer, fire officer etc) do?
- What does each traffic light colour mean?
- Why are there panted lines on the road?
- Why do we have to wear a seatbelt?
- What are street lights for?
- How do we cross the road safely?
- What sort of building do you live in?
- Why do buildings have windows?
- Who designs the buildings?
- If you were designing a building, what would you include in it?

A local artist came to work with the children to develop this masterpiece. The children drew their own house which was transferred onto canvas. Later they were invited to paint their house. Creating a streetscape like this gives the children a great sense of where they belong in the community.

Books to read

Dig Dig Digging by Margaret Mayo
Emergency by Margaret Mayo
Big Blue Train by Julia Jarman
The Journey Home from Grandpa's by Jemma Lumley
The Little Yellow Digger by Betty & Allan Gilderdale. They have also written *The Little Digger at the Zoo*, The *Little Yellow Digger Saves the Whale* and *The Little Yellow Digger and the Bones*.

Chapter 11

Literature

The Gruffalo ~ The Very Hungry Caterpillar ~ Where the Wild Things Are ~ Goldilocks and the Three Bears ~ Wombat Stew ~ Zog ~ Giraffes Can't Dance

In this chapter we show how you can incorporate literature into your program, supporting children as they develop their pre-reading skills and passion for learning. With the right opportunities offered at preschool level, children will start school armed with the skills they require to start reading for themselves.

Use these ideas as a guide and see if you can think of ways of extending or adjusting the experiences to suit the context of the group of children you teach. Refer to chapters 2 and 3 to see how you can support this interest area.

Children's literature is filled with incredible opportunities to develop creativity and imagination and to disappear into a world of make believe. There are many wonderful books that provide opportunities to explore ongoing learning for weeks on end. An entire year's program could be designed based purely on books. Many of the children's picture story books discussed in this chapter have been around to entertain and inspire many generations. Reading books to children helps develop their literacy skills and is said to create a love of learning and a passion for reading. Books will never lose their place in society as long as early childhood educators keep pulling them off the shelves each day and reading with expression, passion and interest. Taking children's minds to another place with the colourful pages, the magnificent words and the places of wonder and delight is one of the greatest gifts we as educators can offer.

Open-ended play spaces

This play space is a set-up of the story of *Goldilocks and the Three Bears*. The CD player behind the mirror plays the story for the children so they can act it out using the props on the table. The activity is designed to support language development and the ability to follow instructions, and has a lovely calming effect, supporting children to regulate their behaviour.

After reading *Polar Bear, Polar Bear What Do You Hear?* the children expressed an interest in polar bears, so we created this play space to support that interest. Individual play spaces like this spark imagination and creativity in children.

Felt storyboards are a fun way to illustrate a story and enable children to demonstrate their memory skills and transference of knowledge. Putting books with the play experiences – in this case *The Three Little Pigs* – allows children to refer to the pictures in the book as they recreate the story.

We have a dog, Lola, who visits our service, and so the children always show a strong interests in dogs. This play experience was in response to that interest and by adding the book *Black Dog* by Pamela Allen, the children can enjoy looking at the story while they play with the dogs.

The story *Owl Babies* by Martin Waddell, is a fabulous extension of children's interest in owls and family. The lovely message that our mummies always come back to us can support the children's emotions and their sense of belonging and attachment.

The stories *The Lighthouse Keeper's Lunch* and *The Lighthouse Keeper's Rescue* are such fun to read at a time when children are interested in the ocean and beach. This set-up enables the children to sort and create patterns.

Here children can support each other in remembering the details of the story, demonstrating their abilities to transfer knowledge from one setting to another, their developing language and communication skills and their ability to negotiate and share ideas.

This experience represents *The Teddy Bears Picnic*. Such play experiences are wonderful for developing creativity, language skills and imagination, and for supporting children in self-regulating behaviour. We have a minimum of three of these experiences in our kindergarten room at any one time.

The children were interested in pyramids so we created this play experience and used the book *Humpty* to support their learning.

Each year someone shows interest in pirates, mermaids and treasure maps. This experience can be created to support that interest. The story *I Wish I Had a Pirate Suit* is a wonderful book to reinforce this interest.

Liam, George and Jacques really enjoyed creating their names out of the letters. This is a wonderful way to support children's developing literacy skills and finding a user-friendly way to start to write our name.

Manipulative play spaces

We made these placemats as the children were developing an interest in writing their names. Before the children arrived we made the letters out of play dough as a stimulus for their play. The children can use the letters in the baskets to make words, spell their name or just to enjoy playing with at the play dough table.

In this experience the children are making gingerbread men out of salt dough. Once they had cut out their shape, we cooked the dough in the microwave. Then the children decorated the men with items from the craft cupboard.

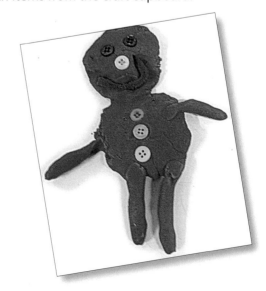

Painting experiences

Each year we frame some of the children's art and exhibit this for family and friends. In this display there are paintings of the Gruffalo, some of the wild things from *Where the Wild Things Are* and butterflies from the *Very Hungry Caterpillar*. We provide pictures for the children to look at and read the stories often, so they become familiar with the characters. Then we invite them to paint and draw their favourite characters. The supporting pictures enable them to focus on details and practise using new skills.

These children are creating very hungry caterpillars using balloons dipped in paint, then decorating them with squeeze paint bottles. This was a lovely follow-on from an interest in creatures from the garden. Experiences such as this have a specific outcome, therefore the children need to follow instructions and use problem-solving skills to work out how to achieve the desired result.

Group projects

This child wanted to draw her favourite princess as she was dressed as a princess that day. She found pictures of princesses on the iPad, so she could focus on the detail that was important to her. The activity helped to develop her fine motor skills and her ability to follow instructions.

We sourced a picture of Elmer the elephant from the internet and printed it on transparency paper then, using an overhead projector we transferred this to a large piece of paper roll. Once the picture is traced the children can paste on various paper and craft items to create the patchwork effect.

Dramatic play

Including drama in your program enables children to take on different roles and explore different identities. It is wonderful for boosting confidence. All children can participate in activities that give opportunities to stand up in front of their friends and express themselves. There are many stories they can act out, both traditional and modern.

With a bit of creativity and innovation you can turn many stories into drama session. Create 'drama bags' that include props you can grab when you decide you would like to do some drama. If they are all ready to go, then they are a fabulous wet day activity.

A puppet theatre is a wonderful opportunity for children to make up their own stories or act out well known stories. It promotes turn-taking, thinking strategies, social skills, concentration and language development.

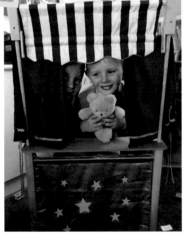

Providing a small puppet theatre for one or two children to use means that the quieter children have an opportunity to express themselves through dramatic play.

Craft experiences

Silly Billy provides a delightful opportunity to discuss our fears and, with the support of the worry dolls, conquer them too. In the book the child is given worry dolls to help him to overcome his fears. You can create worry dolls with the children using wooden pegs, pieces of fabric, pipe cleaners and other craft items. The children then take these home to put under their pillow at night.

We created this teddy bear craft experience after we had a teddy bears picnic at the setting. We read the book, sang the song and then created our own bears to go home. Using a variety of fabrics and paper, these bears are a great way to observe children's spatial awareness and problem-solving skills and their ability to follow instructions.

Sensory experiences

Not everyone feels comfortable using food in early childhood play, and when deciding to do so it is important to take the context of your service into consideration. For example, if you work in an area where families struggle to afford food then you would not use food in your program. It is important to teach children to be responsible and concerned citizens in relation to food, therefore, we teach the children not spill the oats as we will use them again in the future.

This experience is *Goldilocks and the Three Bears*. The play space is set up in a tub with oats in it. Children can recreate the story or simply enjoy the sensory nature of the experience.

Drawing experiences

Providing children with their names, a variety of words, the alphabet and various drawing mediums gives them the opportunity to extend their literacy skills and take on new challenges. Not only does this support children in having a go at writing their own name but it encourages children with increased skills to further extend themselves.

Dressing up the drawing table with items that relate to an area of interest or that support the particular learning goal at the time will encourage children to develop their artistic skills, try new things and add further detail to their art.

The story *Paper Dolls* is the perfect stimulus for creating and decorating these paper dolls. Each child can put their own expression into their dolls. This experience also creates a sense of belonging and develops the concept of community.

Children love writing letters to one another. It is lovely to watch them thinking of their friends, supporting each other's wellbeing and using their developing literacy skills in writing their friends names. The children post the letters either into a letterbox that is emptied each day or into pockets with each child's photo on the front.

Children love to create their own stories. By teaching them about beginning, middle and ending of a story, they can grasp the concept and have a go at writing their own book. Adults can help put the words on each page and the children can do the illustrations. These books can then be read to friends during group times. Expressing ideas develops creativity and imagination.

Cooking experiences

If you read *Possum Magic* you can cook lamingtons or make vegemite sandwiches. If you read *Wombat Stew* you can make your own version of wombat stew, substituting the ingredients of course. If you read the gingerbread man you can cook gingerbread. If you read *The Gruffalo* you can make gruffalo crumble. If you read *Silly Billy* you can make worry doll biscuits. The opportunities are endless. Children love to cook and the combining and mixing of ingredients teaches children about cause and effect and develops their understanding of scientific responses when you combine solids and liquids.

Books to read

All books provide us with something. Some are better than others so when we choose books to read young children we first read them to check that the storyline is appropriate. We also read them so that we know the story. That way we can read with greater expression and ensure that if there are rhyming words we express these well. Reading to children everyday will develop a love of learning, a passion for reading and books and more advanced literacy skills.

The following books are a collection of our favourites:

The Gruffalo by Julia Donaldson
The Gruffalo's Child by Julia Donaldson
Stick Man by Julia Donaldson
Zog by Julia Donaldson
The Very Hungry Caterpillar by Eric Carle
Dear Zoo by Rod Campbell
Where the Wild Things Are by Maurice Sendak
Superworm by Julia Donaldson
Room on the Broom by Julia Donaldson
Fish Out Of Water by Helen Palmer Geisel
The Little Yellow Digger by Betty and Allen Gilderdale
Looking For Crabs by Bruce Whatley

Tiger Who Came to Tea by Judith Kerr
The Smartest Giant in Town by Julia Donaldson
Owl Babies by Martin Waddell
The *Mr McGee* series by Pamela Allen
Silly Billy by Anthony Browne
Paper Dolls by Julia Donaldson
Diggingest Dog by Al Perkins
Hairy Maclary by Lynley Dodd
Greetings from Sandy Beach by Bob Graham
Mog the Cat Series by Judith Kerr
Wombat Stew by Marcia . K Vaughan and Pamela Lofts
Possum Magic by Mem Fox
We're Going on a Bear Hunt by Michael Rosen
Caps for Sale by Esphyr Slobodkina
The Rainbow Fish by Marcus Pfister

Community engagement

Visiting your local library on a regular basis is a terrific way to teach children a love of literature. We visit our local primary school fortnightly and borrow books from their library. This not only supports developing literacy skills but also creates strong bonds with the local school and the children's transition to school is built on a strong foundation. Your local librarian will often be happy to visit the service and read to the children. Advertise for volunteers from a local church or community organisation and ask them to come and read to the children on a regular basis.

Chapter 12

Community, culture and identity

Families ~ Friendships ~ Relationships ~ Traditions ~ Our world ~ Belonging ~ Environment ~ Sustainability

In this chapter we share some of the ways that you can support your service's community and each child's sense of identity.

Use these ideas as a guide and see if you can think of ways of extending or adjusting the experiences to suit the context of the group of children you teach. Refer to chapters 2 and 3 to see how you can support this interest area.

Everyone involved in your service creates the 'community'. This is not just limited to the children in your care, it includes parents, siblings, staff, those involved in excursions/incursions, the surrounding schools, the environment and local services. Community can be explored throughout every play area in your setting. There are creative art and craft experiences, ideas for role play, play dough, drawing and construction, plus wonderful project ideas, incorporating IT, cooking and literacy experiences.

Incorporating the culture of families attending your setting supports the child's sense of wellbeing, their developing identities and their sense of belonging. A family's culture can be experienced throughout your service in cooking experiences, sharing traditional stories, celebrating special days and events and learning about other countries. It is also important to celebrate the culture of the Australian family, sharing food, sharing stories and incorporating the things that are special to each family at your service.

Open-ended play spaces

Creating open ended play spaces based on cultures offers children the opportunity to explore the diversity of people's similarities and differences. Learning from others and respecting other ways of being and doing is a vital step in developing our sense of community. These play experiences were set up to support families in the service.

We used fabric of the table to 'set' the colour scheme of the experience. Aesthetically this is an important base for your play experience, and helps to tie the overall product together. We often use small trinket boxes filled with little treasures such as gemstones or sequins for children to discover and explore. These can be found at discount shops or second-hand shops. Depending on the experience, we also include a lot of small natural items such as gumnuts, leaves, rocks and timber which are all great for enhancing your open ended space.

Chocolate play dough takes the experience to a whole new level. Add chocolate essence, browning essence and cocoa powder to your play dough mixture. This provides children with a sensory experience as it smells like real chocolate. The children can create Easter eggs using the chocolate moulds. We also provide recycled chocolate boxes for the children to make small chocolate treats. Make sure you avoid using chocolate boxes that have contained nuts.

Manipulative play spaces

This pizza play dough was created after a family had come in to make pizzas with the children. We used uncoloured play dough for the pizza 'dough' and for the toppings we used small cut up strips of material to represent ham, tomato, capsicum, olives and cheese. We also provided an oven to cook their pizzas and real pizza cutters.

A lovely experience that helps connect children with the community is to visit your local bakery. You can then extend their learning by creating this bakery play dough experience.

This experience supports our goal for incorporating family cultures into our program and helping children a wider understanding of family values of the people at their service.

The children were invited to draw the houses in their street. Once they had finished the drawing, they added the mosaic squares to represent the roof tiles.

In this experience the children draw the other half of their face. This helps them to develop their power of observation and ability to observe detail. We printed A4 size photos of the children, cut them in half, and stuck one half onto a piece of card. The finished product looks sensational and helps support the children's developing identities.

Another popular play dough experience is to set up an ice-cream shop. This offers children the opportunity to role play and develop their language skills. Here we have used brightly coloured doughs that, when mixed together, will eventually look like 'rainbow' ice-cream. Ice-creams scoops, ice-cream cones (made from roller foam) or cups and toppings like pom-poms, mini umbrellas, buttons and gemstones will keep your ice-cream chefs busy.

Painting experiences

Drawing experiences

Self-portraits are great way of representing each child's identity. Writing and displaying a child's words with their artwork makes them to feel valued and respected. A great way to prompt these words is to ask questions such as *What is your favourite thing to do? What is something you're good at? Who do you like to play with and why?*

Dot painting is one traditional indigenous art method. Show the children some dot paintings and talk to them about how they could achieve the same effect. Providing dot painting examples also helps to make connections between the concept and process. Be mindful of maintaining respect for indigenous culture when participating in experiences such as this.

Group projects

The idea for this experience came from the impact some children's behaviour was having on others in the group. To help them to understand their impact, we needed them to see that they were connected to everyone in the group.

We started with a ball of wool and rolled it across the circle to a child, hanging on to one end of the wool at all times. The child then held the wool and rolled the rest of the ball across the circle to another child. This continued until every child was holding onto the wool.

Once everyone had the wool in their hands we invited one child to gently tug their wool and see that it moved the hands of the other children. We then used the example of using loud voice in the room and that our voices were like the wool and had an impact on other people around us. We then talked about being good friends and that if our behaviour was unpleasant it would have an effect on others. This experience support children to develop a sense of social justice and to understand the effect they have on others. It is a very powerful experience.

Creating murals can be a great way to extend a group interest on a particular topic. After reading the book *Where the Forest Meets the Sea*, we had a group discussion about what could have been at the kindergarten site before it was a kinder. We decided to make the mural in three stages, to illustrate three different eras: bush land, fruit orchards, kindergarten. This helped the children to realise that their environment has changed over time.

As part of this activity, the children had discussions with an aboriginal elder at the botanic gardens about what had existed on the kindergarten land before to the kindergarten.

Sensory experiences

This coffee shop experience can take place in a sandpit, sand kitchen or digging patch – it can get quite messy but also provides lots of fun. Coffee cups, kettles, plungers and real coffee grounds enable the children to create and explore this area using all their sensory capabilities.

Craft experiences

Early in the year, parents are invited to the service to create a special book for their child. This social event not only helps to build relationships between families and the setting, it also helps the child to realise they belong to a family and the community, and fosters their sense of being – engaging in life and knowing who they are.

These 'I love you' books contain photos, poems, pictures, stickers and a visual representation of the child, created with a lot of love by their parents. Children are given these books the following morning at the service and the joy of discovery is shared between the family and their friends.

This experience helps children to learn more about one another and about themselves and their family. The 'I love you' books are kept at the service all year for the children to look at when they want to. It helps them to build the bridge between home and care. The service provides the mini albums, stickers, decorative paper, glue, pens and ideas to help the parents create the book for their child.

Cooking experiences

Inviting families to come and cook a meal from their culture is a great way to include and encourage families to be involved in the program.

Dramatic play

To support children's understanding of the local community we recreated our home corner to represent local services. Fruit shops, bakeries, produce market, doctors surgery, hospitals, vet, post office, restaurant, florist are just a few examples of how you can extend the children learning and understanding of the wider community.

IT activities

Skyping between your setting and another local service helps to develop relationships within the community while also fostering the children's understanding of being part of the community.

To extend this experience you could Skype with the prep teachers from your local primary school or you could even make contact with services from interstate or overseas. This is a great way of sharing ideas and learning from other educators.

Another way to use Skype is to contact family members who are unable to attend special events at your service.

Community engagement

There are many opportunities to engage with your local community. Visits to the post office, fire station, fruit shop, botanic gardens, gallery, farm or bakery are just a few examples. Engaging with the community helps to develop children understanding of the world around them as well as their sense of belonging to being part of the community.

Books to read

The Paper Dolls by Julia Donaldson
Silly Billy by Anthony Brown
Where the Forest Meets the Sea by Jeannie Baker
Big Rain Coming by Karina Germein
It's Okay to be Different by Todd Parr

Reflection questions for group time

- Who are the people in your neighbourhood?
- What does a doctor (vet, baker, etc.) do?
- If there were no postmen (mechanic, firemen, etc.) who would deliver the letters?

Painting

Developing creativity

Children are wonderful to work with in creative experiences as they are (mostly) uninhibited and willing to give new things a try. They go through stages of artistic development that provide them with the skills to draw, paint, build, construct and create. When working with children you will notice them move from scribbling to creating circles and lines and from here they will start to put these shapes together to create recognisable pictures. At this point that you can extend a child's creativity by talking, asking questions, pointing out details and breaking everything they see down to shapes and features that are more manageable for them to replicate in their art.

An example of this is when you want children to try drawing a giraffe. You could put toy giraffes on the drawing table with some props such as logs, grass and rocks. Initially offer only black pen or fine liner.

Sit with the children and talk about the various shapes you can see in the giraffe. *Its tummy looks like a circle or an oval, its neck is like a long line, or two lines side by side. Its head is a smaller oval. Can you see ears and horns on his head? And this giraffe has very long legs.* Then talk about the patterns on the fur. They are like spots but the spots are all different shapes and sizes, and these spots go all the way from his knees to his head.

Once children have drawn the pattern all over their giraffe, you can go on to talk about the details of the hooves, eyes, tail and so on.

This is a task that enables children to use their listening skills, demonstrate their ability to follow instructions and to see that the world around them is made up of shapes that fit together to make up beautiful things, such as giraffes. Children could add colour to their drawings using water colour paints, soft pastels or pencil. However, sometimes those clear black fine line drawings are magnificent just as they are.

Next time you sit with children to draw, say for example a dinosaur, use similar language so that they can see that it's the same shapes just different proportions. *The dinosaur's tummy is an oval, a little like the giraffe we did last month …* The whole animal can be quite daunting which is why we break it down to simpler more shapes.

Marble panting

Once the children master the art of having a go at drawing new things, you can encourage them to add more detail such as grass, sky, sun, ears, eyebrows, teeth, fingers and so on.

In this experience, children create paintings using marbles. We used baking trays lined with white paper and added three main colours. In each colour pot there is a marble which children scoop out with a spoon and placed on the paper. Slowly we pick up the tray and tilt it side to side, and watch how the marbles move over the page. This experience assist with hand–eye coordination and combines art with science as children can explore mixing different colours.

Balloon painting

For this technique, blow up balloons but keep them small so the children can to hold them. Offer two to three colours with a balloon in each, then children dab the balloon onto the paper to create a print. This experience provides a great opportunity to work on colour identification and colour mixing.

Wool painting

Children can make unique works of art by dipping wool into paint. Start by attaching a piece of knitting wool to paddle-pop sticks and dip the wool into a pot of paint. Encourage children to 'dance the wool up and down' over their piece of paper. This shows the children's ability to follow instruction while exploring a new way to be creative and have fun with friends.

Bubble wrap printing

Bubble wrap painting is great way for children to explore textures and create interesting patterns and shapes. Children dip a roller in the paint and then apply it to the bubble wrap. They then turn the bubble wrap over to create a print.

Bubble painting

This bubble painting experience is one of the most popular techniques with children. First mix your paint (non-toxic tempera or food dye). Add a little water and a squirt of washing-up liquid. Stir it and then blow into it using a straw. Before the children begin, get them to practise blowing through the straw onto your hand. Once the bubbles have risen, take a piece of paper and gently press it down over the bubbles. Repeat this process until you have used all the colours. Place on drying rack to dry. This art experience offers a great way to experiment with colour mixing.

Puff painting

Puff painting is a great way to watch paint transform into a 3D form. We mixed one tablespoon of self-raising flour, one tablespoon of salt, some water and a few drops of paint or food colouring. The children began to paint on to their paper or cardboard.

Once they had finished, we placed their painting in the microwave for 30 seconds until the paint puffed. This painting experience gives the children an insight the science or materials.

Finger painting

Finger painting is an excellent tactile-sensory experience that can set up on the table or on a plastic easel. Finger painting stimulates the

children's senses and also teaches them how to mix primary colours and create new ones. It also encourages them to use their imagination and create ... and the best part about it that it's messy and fun.

Instead of using a table or easel, you could also use a ceramic board or a plastic clipboard. Place spoons into the paint containers as this enables the children to scoop the paint out and place it onto the surface. Then their fingers can mix the colours together.

You can also use shaving-foam for finger painting. Squirt the foam onto a table, and then add some colour. Children can mix the colours together and create patterns, words, letters or numbers.

Dropper painting

Using droppers and powder paint, is another great way to explore mixing colours. Adding water to the powder paint transforms into liquid. The children gently squeeze the droppers and observe the colours as they mix together. This supports their fine motor development and is a great science experiment for learning how to mix colours.

Stamping and printing

Stamping is an open-ended art activity and the children can explore using many art materials. You could also use bubble wrap, wooden block stamps, forks, potato mashers, feathers, shells, petals leaves, hands, feet and a variety of other materials.

Children can also explore their senses by creating patterns by painting their feet and gently placing them onto paper to create a print. This is a tactile experience, and also develops language skills as they are learning words such as *wet, squishy, cold, gooey* to describe what they are doing and feeling.

Projector painting

In this experience, the children place their transparency on the overhead projector and paint directly onto it. As they paint, their creation appears on the wall above. It is wonderful to watch the children making the connection between their painting and the image that appears on the wall.

Once these are completed you can display them in a window where the light will shine through them and highlight their work.

Patching

Patching is a stage in of children's artistic development where they create patches or a patchwork effect that covers the entire page. Not all children will go through this stage but those who do will create beautiful works of art as they explore their creativity.

Splat painting

A wonderful a way to involve the reluctant painter is to offer the opportunity to participate in splat painting. Children can throw handfuls of paint at the canvas or paper and watch the dynamic shapes they create. To really make this experience fun, you can put paint into sauce bottles and the children can squirt the paint onto the canvas while it is lying flat.

Canvas painting

Giving children the opportunity to paint onto canvas shows them that we respect them and value their creativity and individuality. Painting onto canvas tends to slow the child down and their painting is more deliberate. It also gives them an opportunity to experiment with different sized paint brushes to provide a different effect.

Easel painting

Easel panting is an amazing opportunity for children to express their feelings, interests, and creativity. Children need opportunities to be able paint and in

Another way to teach the children about famous works of art is to visit an art gallery. Before you go with the children visit the gallery yourself so you can select the works you want to explore with the children. Observe detail such as foreground, middle ground, background, brush strokes and use of colour, and prepare yourself for conversations with the children during the official visit.

order to achieve this goal; they need the freedom to explore the materials and tools. Children are able to explore, mix colours, express themselves, and most importantly use their imagination.

Famous works of art

RED GROUP

'A Very Starry Night'

Exploring famous works of art extends children's knowledge of different ways to paint. In this painting the children explored Van Gogh's *Starry Night* through group discussions and research on the internet. They talked about what they could see in the painting and how Van Gogh might have achieved the swirling effect.

By practising swirling, dotting, and variety of different strokes on easel paper, the children were able to master the brush strokes necessary for recreating the painting. Each child took part in this experience, adding as much or as little as they felt comfortable with.

Taking props that are reflected in the paintings such as real wool if you are looking at *Shearing the Rams* by Tom Roberts, a china tea cup if you're looking at *The Arbour* by Emanuel Phillips Fox or a pair of socks if you're looking at the You Yangs series by Fred William helps the children to engage more deeply with the experience.

Taking small manageable groups means you can give individual attention to each child while also keeping the noise down. Finding out a little history about your chosen paintings, and sharing this with the children makes the experience more valuable.